Contents

Welcome to the United States!

Hello! My name's Benjamin Blog and this is Barko Polo, my **inquisitive** dog. (He's named after ancient ace explorer, **Marco Polo**.) We have just got back from our latest adventure – exploring the United States of America. We put this book together from some of the blog posts we wrote on the way.

Olympic
National Park

CANADA

Glacier
National Park

Great Lakes

CANADA

Columbia
River

Missouri River

Theodore
Roosevelt
National Park

Isle Royale
National Park

Acadia
National
Park

Cascade Range

ROCKY

Columbia Plateau

Yellowstone
National Park

Devils Tower
National Mon.

Mississippi River

Hudson
River

Coast Range

Crater Lake
National Park

Grand Teton
National Park

Badlands
National Park

GREAT

APPALACHIAN MOUNTAINS

Sierra Nevada

Great
Basin

M

Piedmont Plateau

Yosemite
National Park

Arches
National
Park

PLAINS

Ohio River

ATLANTIC COASTAL PLAIN

Zion
National
Park

Mesa Verde
National Park

O

Mammoth Cave
National Park

Death Valley
National Park

Colorado
Plateau

U

Great Smoky Mts.
National Park

Grand Canyon
National Park

N

Arkansas River

Joshua Tree
National Park

Colorado
River

T

Red River

PACIFIC
OCEAN

A

ATLANTIC
OCEAN

I

ARCTIC OCEAN

N

Orlando

RUSSIA

Gates of
the Arctic
Nat'l Park

CANADA

S

Rio Grande

Big Bend
National
Park

GULF COASTAL PLAIN

PACIFIC
OCEAN

Mt. McKinley

MEXICO

Bering
Sea

Denali
National Park

Everglades
National Park

PACIFIC
OCEAN

Gulf of
Mexico

Hawai'i
Volcanoes
Nat'l Park

N
W   E
S

0   150   300 mi.
0   150   300 km

BARKO'S BLOG-TASTIC
UNITED STATES FACTS

The United States is a huge country in North America. On one side of the United States is the Atlantic Ocean and on the other side, the Pacific Ocean. On land, the United States is joined to Canada in the north and Mexico in the south.

5

Story of the United States

Posted by: Ben Blog | 25 May at 2.59 p.m.

The first stop on our tour was Jamestown in the **state** of Virginia. This was where the first English **settlers** built a town in 1607. The *Susan Constant* was one of the ships the settlers sailed in. A copy was made – this is a snap I took of it.

BARKO'S BLOG-TASTIC UNITED STATES FACTS

This is the Lincoln Memorial in Washington DC. Black leader Martin Luther King Jr made a famous speech here in 1963. For years, black people in the United States were treated very unfairly. King told people of his dream that they should be treated equally.

Mountains, rivers, volcanoes and swamps

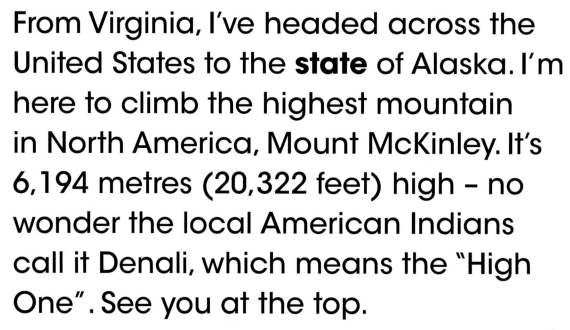

Posted by: Ben Blog | 13 June at 6.23 a.m.

From Virginia, I've headed across the United States to the **state** of Alaska. I'm here to climb the highest mountain in North America, Mount McKinley. It's 6,194 metres (20,322 feet) high – no wonder the local American Indians call it Denali, which means the "High One". See you at the top.

BARKO'S BLOG-TASTIC UNITED STATES FACTS

The Missouri River is the longest river in the United States. It flows for 3,767 kilometres (2,341 miles) from the Rocky Mountains across the centre of the United States and into the Mississippi River near the city of St Louis.

This morning, we arrived in Hawaii, off the south-west coast. Hawaii is a group of islands famous for its volcanoes, and I couldn't wait to explore. Barko took this photo of Kilauea. It has been erupting non-stop for more than 30 years. How amazing is that?

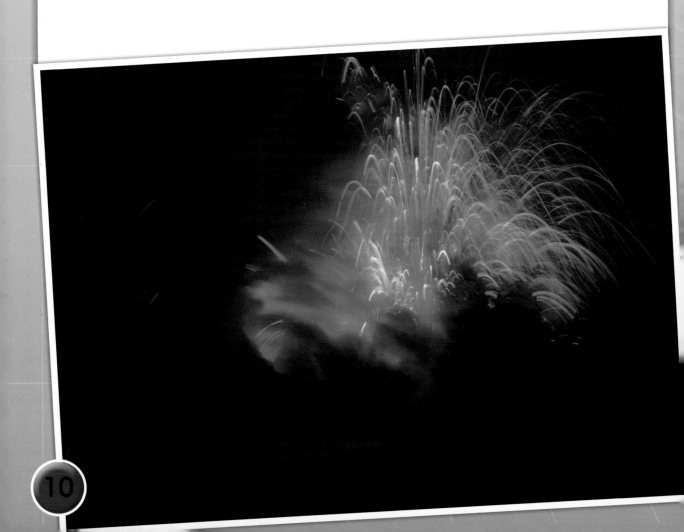

BARKO'S BLOG-TASTIC UNITED STATES FACTS
Huge, marshy swamps cover large parts of Florida. They're called the Everglades. They're home to alligators that can grow up to 4.5 metres (14 feet) long. This one looks hungry, so I'm getting out of its way. Fast.

States and cities

Posted by: Ben Blog | 6 August at 2.11 p.m.

The United States is made up of 50 **states**, including Alaska in the far north and Hawaii in the Pacific Ocean. Our next stop was the city of Washington DC, the capital of the United States. I wanted to see the White House, where the President of the United States lives.

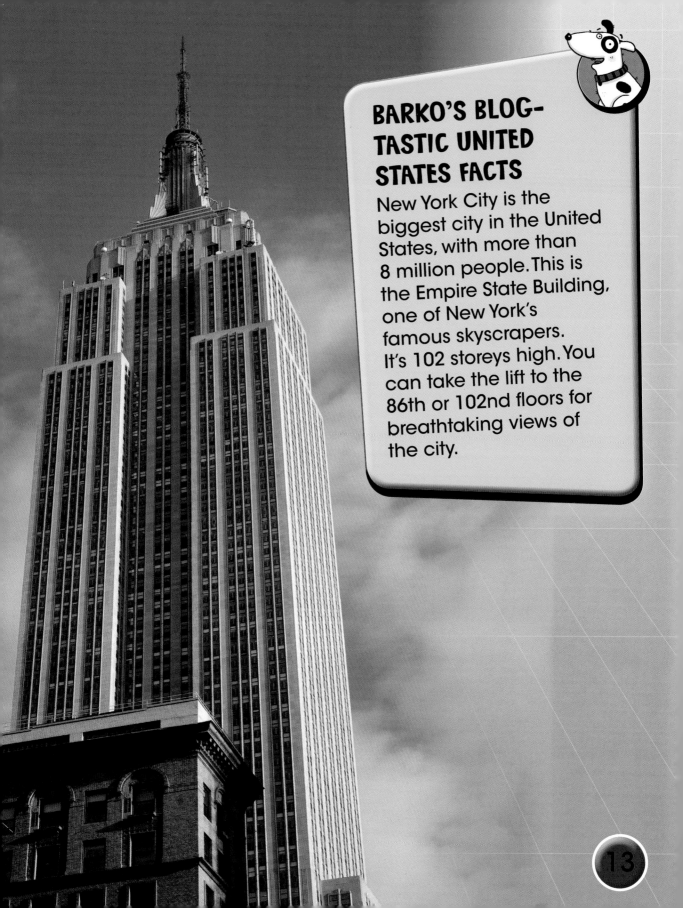

BARKO'S BLOG-TASTIC UNITED STATES FACTS

New York City is the biggest city in the United States, with more than 8 million people. This is the Empire State Building, one of New York's famous skyscrapers. It's 102 storeys high. You can take the lift to the 86th or 102nd floors for breathtaking views of the city.

People of the United States

Posted by: Ben Blog | 20 September at 7.24 p.m.

The first people to live in the United States were American Indians thousands of years ago. The people in the photo are Cherokee Indians. They are wearing traditional clothes. People have come from all over the world to settle in the United States. Today, there are around 318 million people living there.

DANGER

CONSTRUCTION AREA
KEEP OUT

BARKO'S BLOG-TASTIC UNITED STATES FACTS

Most people in the United States speak American English – English, but with many different words and ways of pronouncing them. The second-most used language is Spanish. It is spoken by people whose families came to the United States from Europe, Central and South America. This sign is in both English and Spanish.

SUBSISTENCIA DEL AREA DE LA CONSTRUCCION HACIA FUERA

School and home

Posted by: Ben Blog | 5 October at 9.15 a.m.

American children start school at the age of five years old. This is called **elementary school**. These children are starting their school day by reciting the Pledge of Allegiance. This is a promise to be loyal to their country. They make this promise in front of the American flag.

BARKO'S BLOG-TASTIC UNITED STATES FACTS

Most people in the United States live in big cities. You can travel from city to city by car, aeroplane or train. This is the Empire Builder train on its way from Chicago to Seattle – a 46-hour journey!

17

It's Thanksgiving Day in the United States and everyone's on holiday. This is when families get together and give thanks with a special meal. They eat roast turkey, mashed potato, vegetables and cranberry sauce, with pumpkin pie for pudding. Yummy!

BARKO'S BLOG-TASTIC UNITED STATES FACTS

Many people are Christians but there are many different religions in the United States. This choir is singing **gospel music**. Gospel music was first sung hundreds of years ago in the southern United States. It was sung by African **slaves** as they worked in the fields.

Fast food

Posted by: Ben Blog | 4 December at 12.37 p.m.

American **fast food** is famous all over the world. Here, there are many drive-throughs. A drive-through is a counter where you order your food without having to get out of your car. There are also many **diners** – Barko and I went to one for a hamburger and fries. Think I might try a hot dog next time.

BARKO'S BLOG-TASTIC UNITED STATES FACTS

In the South, people like eating food such as fried chicken, grits (**cornmeal** porridge) and hushpuppies (deep-fried balls of cornmeal). You could also try some Hoppin' John, shown here. It's a dish made from black-eyed peas and rice, with chopped onion and bacon.

Baseball stars to film stars

Posted by: Ben Blog | 2 April at 4.05 p.m.

The next stop on our tour was Boston. I'm here at Fenway Park to watch a game of **baseball**, between the Boston Red Sox and the New York Yankees. Baseball's one of the most popular sports in the United States, and they're two of the oldest and most famous teams.

BARKO'S BLOG-TASTIC UNITED STATES FACTS

This is Hollywood in Los Angeles, California, the centre of the film industry in the United States. Hundreds of films are made here every year. It's a brilliant place to spot some famous film stars. Who's that over there?

From computers to cornfields

From Boston, I travelled west to California to meet up with Barko. I took this snap of Silicon Valley, the centre of the computer industry in the United States. Factories around the United States also make cars, aeroplanes and machinery, making it one of the richest countries in the world.

BARKO'S BLOG-TASTIC UNITED STATES FACTS

There are more than 2 million farms in the United States and most of them are in the Great Plains. This is a vast area of flat land in the middle of the United States. Farmers grow wheat and corn in huge fields. They also keep cattle for their meat and milk.

And finally...

We're nearly at the end of our tour, but we've saved the best for last. We've come to the spectacular Grand **Canyon** in Arizona. It's 445 kilometres (277 miles) long and as deep as four Empire State Buildings. You can hike or climb down. Anyone for a stroll?

BARKO'S BLOG-TASTIC UNITED STATES FACTS

Here in Yellowstone Park, I'm waiting for Old Faithful **geyser** to blow. It's one of hundreds of geysers in the park and the most regular. Old Faithful has gushed up every hour and a half for the last 100 years. Whoa, there it goes...

United States fact file

Area: 9,826,675 square kilometres
  (3,794,101 square miles)

Population: 318,892,000 (2014)

Capital city: Washington DC

Other main cities: New York, Los Angeles, Chicago

Language: English

Main religion: Christianity

Highest mountain: Denali/Mount McKinley
  (6,194 metres/20,322 feet)

Longest river: Missouri River
  (3,767 kilometres/2,341 miles)

Currency: US dollar

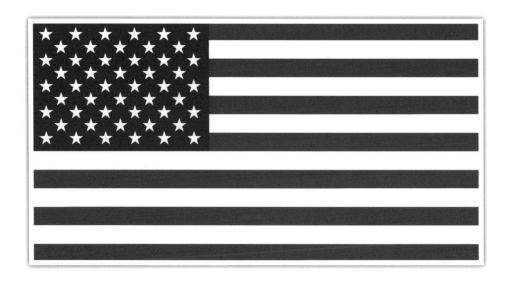

United States quiz

Find out how much you know about the United States with our quick quiz.

1. What is the capital of the United States?
a) New York
b) Los Angeles
c) Washington DC

2. What do most people eat at Thanksgiving?
a) Roast beef
b) Roast turkey
c) Fried chicken

3. Where are films made in the United States?
a) Hollywood
b) Silicon Valley
c) Great Plains

4. How often does Old Faithful erupt?
a) Every three days
b) Every one-and-a-half hours
c) Every five minutes

5. What is this?

Glossary

baseball bat-and-ball game played between two teams who try to score runs

canyon deep gash in Earth's surface, worn out of the rocks by rivers

cornmeal flour made from dried corn (maize)

diner small restaurant with a long counter and booths

elementary school school for children roughly aged between 5 and 12 in the United States

fast food food that is made and served very quickly, such as burgers

geyser huge jet of steam and hot water, heated by volcanic rocks underground

gospel music religious music from the United States, sung by choirs

inquisitive interested in learning about the world

Marco Polo explorer who lived from about 1254 to 1324. He travelled from Italy to China.

settlers people from one country who travel to another country to live

slave person who is owned by another person and works for no payment

state part of a country. The United States has 50 states.

Find out more

Books

The USA (Looking at Countries), Kathleen Pohl (Franklin Watts, 2011)

United States of America (Countries Around the World), Michael Hurley (Raintree, 2012)

USA: Everything you ever wanted to know (Not For Parents) (Lonely Planet, 2013)

Websites

kids.nationalgeographic.co.uk/kids/places/find
National Geographic's website has lots of information, photos and maps of countries around the world.

www.worldatlas.com
Packed with information about different countries, this website has flags, time zones, facts and figures, maps and timelines.

Index